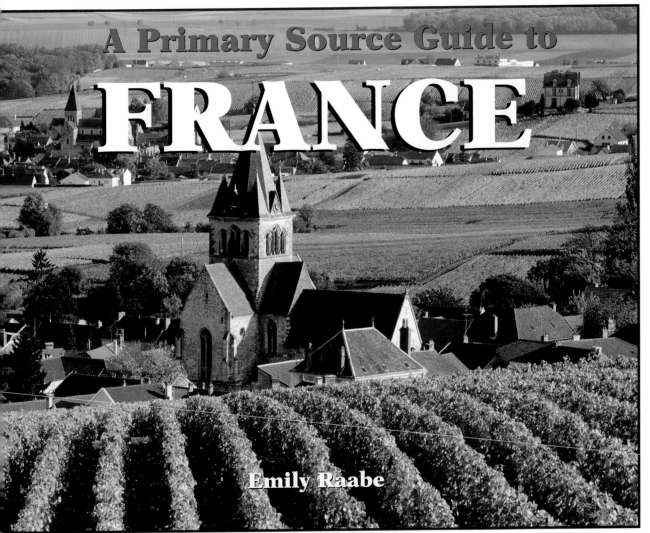

A Primary Source Guide to

FRANCE

Emily Raabe

The Rosen Publishing Group's

PowerKids Press™

PRIMARY SOURCE

New York

To Emma, for whom the world has just begun

Published in 2005 by The Rosen Publishing Group, Inc.
29 East 21st Street, New York, NY 10010

First Edition

Editor: Rachel O'Connor
Book Design: Haley Wilson
Layout Design: Nick Sciacca
Photo Researcher: Adriana Skura

Photo Credits: Cover Image © Georgina Bowater/Corbis; p. 4 © 2002 Geoatlas, (inset) © UPPA/Topham/The Image Works; p. 6 © Ray Juno/Corbis, (inset) © John Noble/Corbis; p. 8 © Christie's Images/Corbis; p. 10 © Gianni Dagli Orti/Corbis, (inset) © Hulton/Archive/Getty Images; p. 12 © Stuart Cohen/The Image Works, (inset) © Amet Jean Pierre/Corbis; p. 14 © Mark Antman/The Image Works; p. 16 © David Sailors/Corbis, (inset) © Mark Antman/The Image Works; p. 18 © Alexander Burakatowski/Corbis; p. 19 © Gianni Giansanti/Corbis Sygma; p. 20 © Owen Franken/Corbis.

Library of Congress Cataloging-in-Publication Data

Raabe, Emily.
A primary source guide to France / Emily Raabe.— 1st ed.
    p. cm. — (Countries of the world, a primary source journey)
Includes bibliographical references and index.
Summary: Text and photographs reveal the culture, history, artifacts, and traditions of France, a nation which is changing but still values its rich history.
ISBN 1-4042-2752-0 (Library Binding)
1. France—Juvenile literature. [1. France.] I. Title. II. Series.
DC17.R33 2005
944—dc22

2003020253

Manufactured in the United States of America

Contents

Atlantic
Ocean

UNITED

IRELAND

KINGDOM

WALES

ENGLAND

NETHERLANDS

GERMANY

BELGIUM

LUXEMBOURG

Paris

FRANCE

SWITZERLAND

ITALY

SPAIN

PORTUGAL

ALGERIA

4

The Many Sides of France

France is the largest country in western Europe. It is 210,026 square miles (543,965 sq km), or about twice the size of the state of Colorado. France is sometimes called the Hexagon because it looks as if it has six sides. It is also bordered by six countries. These countries are Spain, Italy, Switzerland, Luxembourg, Belgium, and Germany. England lies across the English Channel from France. There are more than 60 million people in France. They live in villages, in seaside towns, in the countryside, and in large busy cities such as Paris and Marseille. Paris is France's capital. It has a population of about 11.6 million people.

As you can see from this map, France is larger than any of its neighboring countries. *Inset:* Pictured here is the Eiffel Tower in Paris. The Eiffel Tower is 984 feet (300 m) tall. Visitors can climb to the top and look out over the city.

5

6

Mountains and Beaches

Many parts of France are plains and rolling hills, but there are two mountain ranges in the country. The cold and beautiful mountains known as the Alps separate eastern France from Switzerland and Italy. In the south, the Pyrenees lie between France and Spain. In the center of France there is a **plateau** called the Massif Central. This plateau rises 6,184 feet (1,885 m). It is often windy there. Most of France has cool winters, with **temperatures** around 39°F (4°C). The summers are **mild**, with temperatures around 67°F (19°C). In the south of France, however, temperatures in the summer can be as high as 89°F (32°C). The south is a popular place for people to vacation.

France lies in both northern and southern Europe, which means that its weather varies from hot and dry in the south to cold and snowy in the north. Here is a sunny beach in Nice, in southern France. *Inset:* Skiers enjoy the French Alps.

8

Early France

Many French people are **descendants** of the **Celts**, the Romans, and the **Germanic** tribes that ruled early France. From around 450 B.C. to 58 B.C., the Celts controlled France. The area was then known as Gaul. In 58 B.C., the Romans beat the Celts and ruled France until the fifth century B.C. The Romans brought the Latin language with them. The French that is spoken today comes from both Latin and Celtic. In A.D. 481, Germanic tribes beat the Romans. Later, beginning in 1337, France and England fought several wars over who would control France. This period became known as the Hundred Years' War. The war ended in 1453, when the French drove the English out of France.

France beat England with the help of a teenager named Joan of Arc. Joan was captured and burned to death by the English, but her bravery helped the French to continue their fight. Here is a nineteenth-century painting of Joan of Arc by Dante Gabriel Rossetti.

Revolution

From 1453 until 1789, France was ruled by kings and queens. The citizens did not have any power of their own. This made the French people very unhappy. On July 14, 1789, the French people began a **revolution** that lasted 10 years. The revolutionaries cut off the heads of the king and the queen, Louis XVI and Marie Antoinette. They also beheaded many other people. The revolutionaries created a new flag for France, which is still France's official flag. Today France is a **republic**. The people vote to elect a president every five years. The president appoints a **prime minister** to help run the government.

The storming of the Bastille marked the beginning of the French Revolution in 1789. *Inset:* In 1791 King Louis XVI was forced to sign this document, which ended the church's involvement in government. This helped to ensure that all citizens would be treated equally by the law.

France's Economy

France has one of the strongest **economies** in Europe. France produces many goods such as aircraft, cars, silk, perfumes, and steel. France also produces world-famous wines and cheeses. People around the world buy clothing made by French **designers**. Another big business for France is **tourism**. People come to France to drink wine and to eat delicious food. Of course, they also come to relax and to enjoy the beautiful countryside and the busy cities.

France is a member of the **European Union**, or the EU. France **exports** many of its products, including goods such as wheat and corn, to other countries in the EU, as well as to the United States.

Shown here is the wine-growing area of St. Emilion, a town in the southeast of France. *Inset:* Flowers from all around France are turned into beautiful perfumes in this perfume factory in Provence, in the south of France.

13

14

The French People and Food

The French people are known for their love of good food. In French towns and villages, people buy fresh food every day at outdoor markets and small shops. Even the big cities in France have outdoor markets, where farmers sell fresh vegetables, meat, and fruits.

The usual French breakfast is not large. It may be a croissant or a baguette and a hot chocolate or a large cup of coffee with milk. For most French people, the largest meal of the day is lunch. This meal often consists of a first course, a main course, a salad course, a cheese course, and, last but not least, a dessert course. A lunch like this can take hours to eat!

The French are famous for their loaves of bread, called baguettes. Here a shopkeeper sells her baguettes at a local *boulangerie*, or bakery. Most meals in France are served with baguettes.

15

Paris

Paris is both the capital of France and its largest city. It was built more than 2,000 years ago on an island in the middle of the Seine River. Over time, the city grew too big to fit on the island, so people built on the banks of the river. The area known as the river's Left Bank is the location of the Sorbonne University. This part of Paris has charming streets, small bookstores, and cozy cafés. The Right Bank of the Seine features large shopping malls and many monuments, such as the Eiffel Tower and Notre Dame Cathedral. People who visit Paris often walk along the famous avenue called the Champs Elysées. At the end of the avenue sits the Arc de Triomphe, the largest arch in the world.

Notre Dame Cathedral is more than 800 years old. People come from all over the world to see its gigantic stained-glass windows and beautiful carvings. *Inset:* Shown here is a little book stall on Paris's Left Bank.

18

Artists and Writers in France

Some of the most famous artists in the world come from France. Claude Monet was a famous French **impressionist** painter who  lived during the late 1800s. Impressionist painters painted outdoors instead of indoors. They often painted the same scenes at different times of the day to capture the changing light. Berthe Morisot was another famous French impressionist painter. She often painted pictures of her family members. France has also produced some of the world's most famous writers, such as the poet Charles Baudelaire and the writer Simone de Beauvoir.

This is a famous painting by Monet called *White Water Lilies*. Today you can visit Monet's home and see his gardens in the town of Giverny. *Above:* Simone de Beauvoir sits at a café with her partner, famous writer Jean-Paul Sartre.

20

Old Ways, New Ways

France is famous all over the world for being a leader in fashion, art, **literature**, and wonderful food. However, even as they look to the  future, the French do not forget their **traditions** and roots. For example, the old French money, the franc, has been replaced by the European Euro. However, the French language is the same as it has been for hundreds of years. French people are very proud of their language and guard it carefully to make sure that it remains traditional. This beautiful country has managed to change with the times while remaining true to its own French traditions, language, and pride.

In this Bastille Day Parade, people dress in the costumes, or clothing, of 1789 when the French Revolution began. *Above:* France started using the Euro on January 1, 2002.

France at a Glance

Population: 60,180,529

Capital City: Paris, population about 11,600,000

Official Language: French

Official Name: The French Republic

National Anthem: "La Marseillaise" ("The Song of the Marseille")

Government: Democratic Republic

Unit of Money: Euro

Land Area: 210,026 square miles (543,965 sq km)

Flag: The flag is divided into three equal stripes of red, white, and blue. The blue and red stripes are the colors of Paris and the white is the color of the king. The flag was created after the French Revolution.

Glossary

Celts (KELTS) Early European people who lived in the British Isles, France, Spain, and parts of Asia.

descendants (dih-SEN-dents) People born of a certain family or group.

designers (dih-ZY-nurz) People who create plans for a new product.

economies (ih-KAH-nuh-meez) The ways in which countries or businesses manage their supplies and energy sources.

European Union (yur-uh-PEE-in YOON-yun) A group of countries in Europe that work together to be friendly and to better their businesses.

exports (ek-SPORTS) Sends something to another place to be sold.

Germanic (jer-MA-nik) Relating to German-speaking people.

impressionist (im-PREH-shuh-nist) Relating to a style of art in which the subject is not as important as how the artist uses color and tone.

literature (LIH-tuh-ruh-chur) Writings such as novels, plays, and poetry.

mild (MYLD) Gentle or calm.

plateau (pla-TOH) A broad, flat, high piece of land.

prime minister (PRYM MIH-nih-ster) The leader of a government.

republic (ree-PUB-lik) A form of government in which the authority belongs to the people.

revolution (reh-vuh-LOO-shun) A complete change in government.

temperatures (TEM-pruh-cherz) How hot or cold things are.

tourism (TUR-ih-zem) A business that deals with people who travel.

traditions (truh-DIH-shunz) Ways of doing things that have been passed down over time.

23

Index

Primary Source List

Cover. Vineyards in Champagne, France. 1999. Photograph by Georgina Bowater.

Page 6. Sunbathers on a beach in Nice, on France's Cote d'Azur. Circa 1980s–1990s. Photograph by Nik Wheeler.

Page 6 (inset). Skiers near the resort of Chamonix in the French Alps. Circa 1970–1974. Photograph by John Noble.

Page 8. *Joan of Arc Kissing the Sword of Deliverance* by Dante Gabriel Rossetti. Circa 1845.

Page 10. *Storming of the Bastille* by Jean-Pierre Houel. 1789.

Page 10 (inset). The French constitution, dated September 3, 1791. King Louis XVI's signature is in the left-hand margin.

Page 12 (inset). Perfume production at a factory in Grasse, Provence. 1995. Photograph by Jean Pierre Amet.

Page 16. Notre Dame Cathedral. Paris, France. 2001. Photograph by David Sailors.

Page 18. *White Water Lilies* by Claude Monet. 1899.

Page 19. Jean-Paul Sartre and Simone de Beauvoir at a café in Rome. 1978.

Page 20. Two drummers in period costume participate in the Bastille Day parade for the bicentennial of the French Revolution. July 14, 1989. Photograph by Owen Franken.

Web Sites

Due to the changing nature of Internet links, PowerKids Press has developed an online list of Web sites related to the subject of this book. This site is updated regularly. Please use this link to access the list:

www.powerkidslinks.com/cwpsj/psfran/